In *Orange Tulips*, Joan Barasovska explores the perilou̶ woman, she was "neither dead nor safe." We follow ̶ lethal precipices of her own mind, then into locked psychiatric wards, where she battles a "death sentence [that] glares from both sides" of her family tree. In the halls of madness, she finds herself writing down the "accidental poetry/of overheard hallucinations." These are brave poems, unflinching in their examination of a period of near self-destruction in the poet's life. These are also poems that relish "the ecstatic lift/of strength and artifice" that poetry-making contributes to the difficult work of becoming who we are. A triumphant Barasovska emerges in these pages, enjoining us to "Admire me in my bikini on the high dive / blindfolded and in love at the same time." And admire her we do, for being so in love with poetry that she saved her life.

—Victoria Reynolds, Ph.D., clinical psychologist and poet

Joan Barasovska's debut collection, *Birthing Age*, introduced us to an intelligent and moving poet. *Orange Tulips* meets and surpasses that achievement. Embedded in this full-length collection is a kind of *bildungsroman*, an account in verse of the poet's passage through the "unfurled song" of infancy and childhood to the trial-by-fire attainment of adult agency. At the center of the poet's remarkable story is her late childhood, adolescent, and young adult struggle with mental illness. "Nothing lifts the darkness she's in," says the poet of her eleven-year-old self. Ultimately victorious, the emergent woman comes to "love this world [she] yearned to shed." From the bravura realism of "The Penn Fruit" to the Dickinsonesque lyricism of "Romance," *Orange Tulips* reminds us that a full life is always a story of valor and generous love.

—Maria Rouphail, Ph.D., author of *Apertures*, *Second Skin*, and *All the Way to China*; poetry editor at *Main Street Rag*

The poems in Joan Barasovska's *Orange Tulips* are so powerfully teeming with visceral life, the inattentive reader might be forgiven for overlooking their consummate craft. Each poem in this collection is distinguished by the honesty of its details, its fully-rendered tone, and its careful formal design. The book itself is just that: a *book*, each of whose poems adds to the unfolding arc of narrative, never belabored but always fully present, anchoring and enlarging the individual utterances, until the whole is indeed larger than the sum of its parts. The thrill of reading *Orange Tulips* is multi-dimensional: Each poem stands on its own, but each participates in the unfolding narrative. Here are rage and grief, loss and pure bewilderment, enacted through a lens of honesty and love. *Orange Tulips* is a significant achievement.

—Michael Hettich, author of *Systems of Vanishing*, *The Frozen Harbor*, *Bluer and More Vast*, *To Start an Orchard*, *The Mica Mine*

Other Works

Birthing Age (Finishing Line Press, 2018)

Carrying Clare (Main Street Rag, 2022)

ORANGE TULIPS

poems

Joan Barasovska

REDHAWK
PUBLICATIONS

Redhawk Publications
The Catawba Valley Community College Press
2550 US Hwy 70 SE
Hickory NC 28602

ISBN: 978-1-952485-37-4

Library of Congress Control Number: 2022940583

Cover photo (the author at sixteen): Frank Gruber,
with his permission

Author photo: Hannah Kitchin Stewart

*Time tells me what I am. I change
and I am the same.
I empty myself of my life and my
life remains.*

—Mark Strand

for my parents

Elsie Nax Freeman (1919-2013)
Bernard Freeman (1921-2002)

Contents

Only Now

Word by Word

poems are
houses I build
a town
line by line

each dwelling
a home
to a poem
I create

with the tools
in my hands
I invent
what I know

the words
blow away
the town
stands below

TOO YOUNG

I still follow the child who walks inside me.

—Adonis, translated by Khaled Mattawa

In the Belly of a Rose

in the belly of a rose
curls my waiting

red is the rose
swelled by such fruit

bright are the petals
spiraling the core

my unfurled song
child of perfect wait

Lullaby

much-wanted
long-carried
milk-lapped
moon-perfect
winter baby
solstice girl
basin-bathed
mother-soothed
father-loved
cradle-rocked
sleep child
sleep

His Heart

Small girl and father
side by side on her parents' bed
Daddy in striped pajamas
weeks after the hospital
his prickly face, his curly chest
she pets his hand, this worried child.

Baby Mike sleeps in his crib
too young to know Daddy is sick.
Daddy's big hands, his brown eyes
she wants to keep him, to feed him
a girl of four who can't help much.

Gramom Elizabeth takes the bus
across town to cook and help with Mike.
Sister hears tight voices in the kitchen
Yiddish words she doesn't know.
Mommy carries a tray to the bedroom
chicken soup, iced tea in a foggy glass.

No one says Daddy will wear a suit
again, no one thinks she understands,
small child too small to help him
she longs for magic to make him strong
his healing heart to keep her safe.

St. James Street
for Christine

the slate sidewalk in front of my house
where we jumped rope, chalked hopscotch
games and threw the stones that marked
our shaky one-foot turns, spun hula hoops
around our skinny waists until they crashed,
yours before mine, mine before yours,
and we bounced a small white ball to a song
that timed a story, one-two-three-alaree,
four-five-six-alaree, and the slate answered true,
and it blackened with raindrops and burned
with summer, and we took turns on stilts,
and spun off on zinging roller skates.
I try to remember it all, I can't remember it all.

The Penn Fruit

At my mother Elsie's side, left hand resting
on the cool metal of the cart, I am her young
apprentice at The Penn Fruit. She makes me
sniff a giant pineapple which she puts back,
selects a fragrant one, settles it in the cart.
The bananas she picks are streaked with green.
She tells me why. Oranges can't have squishy
soft spots. She shows me brown bruises
on the Red Delicious apples she puts back;
she chooses a half dozen Winesaps for a pie.
We'll need a can of Crisco for the crust.
Iceberg lettuce, carrots, turnips, celery.

I dread the butcher counter, the raw red meat,
the chalky fat and bones looking too much
like what they are. My mother, always strict
with me and now with the butcher, demands
he grind beef just for her. He weighs and wraps up
lamb chops, steak. She'll buy her fish
at Reading Terminal, her chicken and eggs
from the farmer who rings the doorbell Friday nights.
I heard my mother tell my dad the farmer
has liquor on his breath. I'm not sure what's wrong
with that, I like the farmer and his truck,
a grinning pig painted on its side.

We need Kaiser rolls, Grossinger's seeded rye,
Kellogg's corn flakes, Philadelphia cream cheese,
cheddar cheese, an icy jar of Vita pickled herring
for my father. Milk is too heavy to wheel home,
we'll buy more at Shain's tomorrow. Little cans
of frozen orange juice, blocks of icy spinach,
Breyer's chocolate ice cream. I stack them
neatly in the cart. Stewed tomatoes, mandarin
oranges delicate as doll food, Campbell's soup,

16

sardines. Gulden's mustard, peanut butter,
Tide detergent in a box, blue Scott toilet paper,
Clorox bleach. I'm watching, I'm listening,
this is serious, this is women's business.

At the deli counter my mother holds the little
cardboard number she yanked from the machine
and I'm allowed to tip back the hinged cover
of the wooden pickle barrel, reach down
into the aromatic brine with metal tongs,
pull out my dripping prize. My mother helps me
slide it into its waxed paper bag. I nibble
on its sourness while she orders a quarter-pound
of muenster cheese, a half-a-pound each of turkey
and roast beef, *rare*, all of these sliced *thin*.
While we wait there's a neighbor lady
my mother is polite to. I can tell they don't like
each other much. My mother should be nicer.

Our cart's piled high. I help her load our groceries
onto the narrow moving belt. It takes so long to ring
it up, to count the change, to stack our things
in six brown paper bags, which the bagger boy
piles for us in our wheeled cart. I will help
my mother pull our heavy groceries eight blocks
home from Market at 19th to 23rd and St James.
I will help her bump the cart up the steep front
granite steps, though I am only seven. Together we will
put away each can and box and bottle, apple, onion,
brown butcher package, each in its own special place.

5905 Belmar Terrace

Mike and me sit in Gramom Elizabeth's kitchen,
elbows on oilcloth. Gramom gives us chicken soup
with kneidlach. She's made kotleten because
she knows I love them, and kasha mit varnishkes.
There's sliced tomatoes, cucumbers, and challah.
For dessert there's ice cream sandwiches
we dug out of the freezer at Frank's Grocery.

We're sleeping over at Gramom's Saturday night
so Mom and Dad can stay out late without a babysitter.
This morning I named the flowers in Gramom's garden:
hydrangea, zinnia, snapdragon, gladiola, and everyone
knows roses. Gramom got down on her knees
on newspaper to pull out weeds. I helped her water.

It's summer now, but on New Year's Eve when
we sleep over, Gramom wakes us up for midnight
and puts us in our coats. We stand on her stoop
to bang on pots with wooden spoons and watch
the bad boys down the block set off firecrackers.
Today she took us down the hill to Cobbs Creek Park,
a steep walk back but we tried not to whine.

There's a skylight in her bathroom with a long chain.
The bathtub is very deep and stands on curvy feet.
Even though I know how to do it now,
Gramom washes me with a washrag and Sweetheart
soap just like she washes Mike. She scrubs our dirty
knees and elbows hard because she's very strong.

We are her Joanele and Mikele, her kinderlach.
We sleep together in the big bed in the front room.
Gramom tucks us in between thick white sheets.
Her blue eyes smile behind her spectacles.
She sings a Yiddish song. The giant mint leaf of the
Breyer's sign on Frank's Grocery is our nightlight.

Recital

Two by two across the stage,
barefoot girls in promenade,
two straight lines, arms linked just so,
prancing steps, pointed toes.

Mrs. Blank begins the story
of *Madeline*, told in rhyme:
*In an old house in Paris
that was covered with vines...*

One child, in thrall to grace and rhythm,
drilled in effortless precision,
marks her cues, obeys the music,
weaves a way across the boards.

Watch her spin, intake of breath,
unbroken smile, ecstatic lift
of strength and artifice,
first grasp of beauty's hold.

Twelve little girls in two straight lines,
in black leotards and pale pink tights,
one amongst them lit by glory,
inside a Saturday, inside a story.

Sore Throat

The best light in our rowhouse on St. James Street
is from the tall front windows in the living room.
I wait by the window in my pajamas for Dr. Barol
to ring the doorbell and for his jolly voice.
I'm to sit on the piano bench where he can see best,
his black leather bag beside me, its jaw wide open.
He stands above me in horn-rimmed glasses and bow tie,
shakes down the mercury in his glass thermometer.
He tells me to say *AH* and says, *Open wide.*
My tonsils are infected again, he tells my mother.

I want him to convince her to pity me.
Tell her I must stay in bed for a week.
Tell her to be nicer when she talks to me.
Please don't tell my mother that sickness
is what I crave most of all.
I'm sure he can tell. He's shined a light
in my throat and ears so many times
he must know my trick.
I'm a little girl who believes she can
make herself sick just by being sad.

The nurse at school, Mrs. Marx, knows me well.
She rolls crinkly paper down the padded leather
table so I can rest with her if no one else is there.
She plays the opera music she loves on her radio.
I know she knows my secret, but maybe
she forgives me. From the bottom of my being
I want the gentleness that only sickness gets you.

But it doesn't really work that way.
My throat is so sore. My mother's angry
that I'm sick again. She has too much to do.
She makes me Cream of Wheat
with brown sugar. She pours medicine
from a brown bottle into a spoon.
She takes my temperature, gives me baby aspirin,
puts cool washcloths on my forehead, changes
the sheets. She does all that she should do.
I need what I can't name.

Betsy McCall

Betsy has a sweet pink smile,
stiff honey-colored hair, eyelids
that close when I lay her down to sleep
and tuck her in with a scrap of Mike's
blue baby blanket. Her knees bend
to sit in her red wooden chair.
She drinks from a tiny tea cup
with pink rosebuds. She plays
with blocks and her own little doll.

I speak Betsy's voice for the stories
I make up. Things happen that I don't
expect. She gets sick a lot and rides
to the hospital in an ambulance.
Sometimes she's a second-grade
teacher and all the kids love her.
Sometimes in Family everyone
is happy, some days the mother is mad.

I don't know if Betsy is my little girl
or my sister or my friend.
She sits in my hand, tilts her head,
smiles into my eyes.

Physics

a rectangle
like a dining table
but a trick table
weighted at one end
like a seesaw
mother holding down
the strong seat
sister and brother
like a fulcrum
locked in stasis
father dangling
from the high seat
denied gravity
a system
an experiment
in force

My Little Brother

I remember Mike and me in twin beds
in the front room facing the street.
When Mom turned off the light,
we began our Evening Chat.
When we carried on too late
Mom would yell up the stairs,
Cut it out!
We yelled back in unison,
With a scissors and paper?

We invented Gravy Train,
a cube-shaped planet
that spun around the Earth.
On each side lived a different species,
but now we remember only two:
bunyips (mythical seal/dog creatures)
and aproned grandmothers,
each species happy to inhabit
its own side of a new planet.

The *Playboy* magazine we peeked at
in the tenants' stack of mail
was the model for our own edition,
silly dirty jokes illustrated with betsies
and petsies, poopies and pee pee,
crayon and pencil on construction paper,
bound proudly with brass fasteners.

Saturday mornings we made a racket
moving our furniture around.
How many ways could there be
to arrange two twin beds, one nightstand,
one bureau, one little bookcase?
Mike and I tried them all.

He told me years ago when I was sad
that he always thought of us
as special, better than anyone else.
Brother and sister, sister and brother,
the ones who understand the way it was.
The band of us, the bond of us, just us.

Freeman's Suits Coats and Dresses

Mike and I swing a heavy horseshoe magnet
on a rope to pick up straight pins stuck
in the carpet of Daddy's store, pins scattered
around three-way mirrors near the dressing
rooms where ladies in outfits pose while
girls from the backroom crouch with pins
in nipped lips to tack up hems and sleeves.

Racks of dresses hang, flowery polished
cotton frocks in spring, coats with wide
collars and shoulder pads, shirtwaist
dresses, gowns in glittery colors, pastel
Easter suits and tweed suits with flaring
peplums. I know the words, I whisper
them and stroke the fabrics.

At the entrance greeting customers,
Betty the milliner stands behind her
counter. Sparkly costume jewelry,
leather gloves and evening purses
are on display. She decorates a hat:
cluster of cherries on a straw brim,
feathers on a felt cloche, jeweled pin
for a pillbox with a veil.

In the noisy backroom Joe Forlani is the boss.
He's the tailor, in charge of the seamstresses,
his girls, at their machines doing alterations.
He wears a tape measure around his neck
and tailor's chalk behind his ear.
Joe made me a wool pleated skirt in red,
my favorite color. He sings *Volaré*,
oh-oh-oh-oh, cantaré for us.

Salesgirls help the customers search
the racks. They pull out dresses and hang
them in the dressing rooms, where ladies
in bras and girdles, garters and stockings,
lacy slips, try on dresses, part the curtains,
twirl in front of mirrors to see what fits,
what the salesgirls think looks best.

And everywhere I see my father,
Buddy, in a fine suit, silk tie, French cuffs
with monogrammed gold cufflinks,
shoes buffed to a high shine. At home
I help him with the shoeshine kit.
He lets me watch him shave, his brush
in a flowered china mug with his father's
name on it. I pick out his ties and tie tacks.
I'm certain everyone in the store loves him,
the way they joke and laugh together.

At Christmastime Daddy treats the family
and the people from the store to lunch
at Pub Tiki, where frowning gods guard
the door. I sit between my mother
and Betty the milliner. Underneath palm trees
we eat food stuck on skewers and served
on a giant Lazy Susan. Betty asks me
what I'll be when I grow up. I say, *an actress.*
Daddy smiles at me across the table.

The Huckster

You don't want that cantaloupe, Mrs. Freeman,
smell this honeydew! Sweet and juicy!
Mom and me are standing outside Rago's truck
early Saturday morning before it gets too hot.
He's parked at his Saturday spot at 22nd and Locust.
Neighborhood ladies with wheeled carts like ours
are crowded around crates of fruit and vegetables,
squeezing, smelling, sliding their choices into bags.
My mother wears a housedress and flip-flops.
I'm wearing my YWCA Sum-Fun Day Camp T-shirt.

I like the huckster in his dirty apron.
He hands me green paper that wrapped one pear
because he knows I love to sniff the flowery smell.
He weighs each bag on the tippy scale that hangs
from a roof he props up for shade.
He piles dollar bills and drops coins in a metal box.
His hands are rough and hard.
Brown bags of plums, pears, grapes, peaches,
carrots with their greens pile up in our cart.

Grazie, says Mr. Rago as Mom counts out her pennies.
Arrivederci, says my mother as we turn and wheel away.

Choking

I clutch the pool's rim, bangs dripping,
face convulsed by coughing, spitting,
in the din of the YWCA pool.
The other girls in the Minnows Class
are swimming laps I should be swimming.

Coach Susan stares down at me.
She knows I didn't swallow water.
She's angry but I can't stop
pulling over to grant myself reprieve,
to leave my lane and rest.

Arm over arm the Minnows churn,
treading their paths between the ropes.
I perch on the ledge, disgraced but safe
from the strangling symmetry of this place.

Found Magic

He was a wooden block, a triangle
with worn-down points. I don't remember
where we found Oglethorpe or who named him.
Leslie drew eyes inside round spectacles
and a smile with black crayon. We hid him
in a shoebox in my bureau's bottom drawer.

Oglethorpe was waiting for us the next day.
We shut the door to keep out nonbelievers
like our brothers. Leslie made up magic words
to whisper when we touched him.
I made up arcane ceremonies of obeisance.

Puck was a tin of blue paint popped from a child's
watercolor set, a little dirty and used-up. I spotted
her in the gutter on Ranstead Street behind Leslie's
block of Spruce. We dared not clean her paint.
Leslie and I knew magic when we saw it.

Puck and Oglethorpe, potent and complete,
swaddled in white tissue from a Gimbel's bag,
waited in their shoebox in the drawer.
Incantations were recited with stifled giggles.
Did we make wishes? What we wished for
was a sign, and it had been doubly granted to us.

Leslie died the summer we were fifteen.
An illness no one named stole her away
and I am free to tell our story. I can see us
hunkered down on Ranstead Street, dirty knees,
flushed cheeks, dusting off our brilliant secret.

1963

I'm a merry Girl Scout in green uniform
and felt berct. My troop is walking east across
the Schuykill River Bridge. It's an old bridge,
prickly sandstone under our palms.

You can sit on the ledge if you're brave.
You can stand on the ledge if you're foolish.
We look between the columns way down to the water.
How deep is it? Miss Kelly doesn't know.

What I care about, in one breath, is the impact of a fall.
The magnet of the gray river. The sick.
I don't ask Miss Kelly why people jump.
She knows about hikes, knots, campfires.
Starting today, I'm the authority on jumping.

Merit badges, saddle shoes, jokes I am famous for.
I am nine, maybe ten.
Now I have a secret so strong it makes me dizzy.
On my honor, for God and my country,
it's 1963 and I have fallen down.

Girl on a Bus

She sits in the back row
of the number 17 bus,
her cheek cool against the glass.
She can't know why
she's cried all day at school.
She starts crying again
just wondering why.
Nothing lifts the darkness she's in.
She's written a poem about hope,
the word itself a talisman
to hold until this passes,
as quickly as it descended.

She is not to know, at eleven,
that this time is only the first.
Her life will be marked
by deep troughs,
years just like this month
she has no word for.
She will be a teenager
in a car, a young woman
in a hospital, a wife,
a mother, her cheek cool
against the glass,
wondering when it will
end this time, this time.

The sad girl pulls a cord
signaling the driver
to stop at Walnut Street.
She walks a block to catch
the number 42 that will
take her to her quiet house.
The world looks dark
and inexplicable
to this child in tears.
She rings the bell.

You're So Beautiful

My family prized humility.
Compliments were nonsense
to be flicked aside.
My mother thought herself plain,
too fat, her nose too big, she waved off
Dad's camera, wouldn't smile.

But even Mom once said that everywhere
we went people stared at me.
When her friend Ethel painted my portrait
in somber blues and grays, I was ten.
Ethel often sketched me in charcoal,
saying, *You're so beautiful.*

You're so beautiful.
My girlfriends said it, teachers too,
my parents' friends, and cousins,
strangers, and then boys.

Where was this beauty, invisible to me?
I stared at the mirror over the sink,
the girl I studied not the one transmuted
by the alchemy of others' eyes.

First Date

Charles McKinney asked me out! Leslie can't
believe it. We shriek on the phone, *He's sixteen!*
We're fourteen. Leslie has never been asked.
I met Charlie at Lloyd's party. *No, he's not
like Lloyd, he wasn't drinking beer.*

My mother is thrilled. We're going ice-skating
at the Penn Center Rink. He'll see how graceful
I am! At the party he said he likes my long hair.
I'll wear it loose and braid it for the ice.
Leslie and I study at The Academy of Seventeen
Magazine. We choose Yardley lip gloss, Maybelline
eyeliner and blush, Muguet de Bois cologne by Coty.
Will he kiss me goodnight? Will he ask me out again?

The night of the date it's raining so the rink is closed.
Now it's a bowling date. Charlie shakes my parents'
hands in the front hallway. He's taller than my dad.
Mom beams up at him, tells him my curfew is 10:00.
We walk to Penn Center Bowling on Market Street.
I'm proud to walk beside a boy who's big as a man.

Bowling isn't nearly as good as skating for showing off.
I'm terrible at it, my hands are sweaty and I can't
remember how to keep score. I watch him take his turns
and wonder what to say on the walk home. We stop
for Cokes and burgers at Dewey's. He pays for everything
like he's supposed to. When will he ask me out again?

He says his parents want to meet me. That's a good sign!
No one's home. Sweat trickles down my sides. *Let's sit
and talk on the couch. I like talking to you.* His tongue jams
into my mouth, his hands squeeze my breasts, he shoves
his knee into my crotch in a rush of force I push against,
push against, pull hard away to stand.

First Love

Doug was eighteen, gangly, tall, with freckles
and wild black curls. At camp we lay on a hillside
pasture pleasuring each other. We sat on the backstairs
of my cabin, me in a pale pink nightgown, unbuttoned
so he could kiss my breasts, I could kiss his hair.
We were a couple, he a junior counselor, me a camper.

Letters, dozens of letters, from Philly to Queens
and back again, his in a whimsical hand. His laughter
on long distance calls, Greyhound Bus to Port Authority
when I had the babysitting cash. We walked all day,
ate huge sandwiches in delis, made out in Central Park,
bought five-dollar SRO tickets to Broadway shows,
sang show tunes on Manhattan streets: *Camelot,
Man of La Mancha, Zorba, Charlie Brown.*

We had all night in a bedroom in our friend Susie's
Riverside Drive apartment while her parents were away,
a whole night in his arms. He took hours to gently open me,
lovingly. He slid inside, eager and exhausted, laughing,
glad, and I, bloody and undone at sixteen, was relieved.

The next day Susie the ballerina, Doug and I walked
winter streets eating roasted chestnuts, leaping curbs.
Susie was proud to be the host of our first lovemaking.
I was startled by hot fluid down my thighs—more blood?
Doug whispered and we laughed.

Lucky, lucky girl to have as my first lover a boy crazy
in love with me, a boy I was crazy about, who knew
what he was doing and had nothing to prove,
to wake with his kisses on my eyelids
and walk city streets beside him, holding hands,
clicking heels, and laughing in defiance of the rules.

ALL WRONG

I remember madness leaning for the first time on the mind's pillow.

—Vincent van Gogh

A Dark Door Opens

Alone at night in the backseat
of a stranger's car going back to college
the Sunday after Thanksgiving,
I see a row of shiny knives that are not there.
I want to die immediately, I need to die.
I am eighteen, nearly nineteen.
I can't sit still in this car.
There's no way to die in here.
I want the car to crash right now.

In my dorm room I hide in bed.
My roommate brings me food,
she tries to make me eat.
I go to a few classes
but only hear a roaring sound.
Tree roots on the sidewalk
want to make me fall.
My bewildered father drives up,
packs my things and takes me home.
I can barely talk. Time has slowed.
I ask my mother to hide the kitchen knives.
She refuses, but I don't have the guts
to use sharp things. Not yet.

They send me to an analyst,
but I don't trust him.
I lie on his leather couch
four times a week, hardly speaking.
At midnight on New Year's Eve,
my parents at a party, I throw
myself down the basement stairs.
I stand up bruised in the dark basement
without a plan. I tell no one.
I don't belong on the street.
It's a bitter winter and I walk and walk.

One day, everyone at work,
I take all the pills in my parents'
medicine cabinet and lie down
on the grey carpet beside their bed
but lose my nerve and ring the
neighbors' doorbell.

An ambulance, my stomach pumped.
My mother appears in the ER, so angry.
For days my ears ring
from handfuls of aspirin I swallowed,
filling and filling the pink plastic cup.

I keep walking. I have a boyfriend
but love doesn't help, nor does spring.
All summer I work a clerical job
on the 31st floor of an insurance building,
but as I answer desperate calls
from widows and promise
that the check is in the mail,
I'm drawn to the shiny
floor-to-ceiling windows
lining the far wall.

Waking at Noon

split wires
cold sweat
dark day

singed fingers
forced socket
short circuit

failed nerve
high voltage
all broken

bad electrician
poor training
no license

no current
no charge
blackout

All Wrong

Done so many things wrong
I don't know if I can do right.
                    —Tracy Chapman

The built world defeats me.
My apartment, the building
where I answer phones,
the sidewalks I walk on,
have all done great things
to my nothing at all.

If I were in charge
this city would be empty,
wind blowing soot.
Just look at me!
A shanda, disgrace,
such a smart girl,
dropout, breakdown,
breakup, crackup.

I am twenty.
I read long novels.
I walk and walk.
I only feel well
on trains and buses.
I draw odd diagrams
in small books.
I don't wonder
why I'm done for.

I only want to be
as useful as a sidewalk,
to hammer one nail straight.

Happy twenty-first

to this lucky young woman with green cat's eyes
and a red, green, yellow checked shirt
with mother-of-pearl snap buttons.

She shouldn't be that thin, a girl like this one,
brought up to take care of herself.
Her hair could be cleaner, her skin is splotchy.

It's a crowded room, but not a party room,
it's an elevator going up to the fifth floor,
and her parents are there, and a resident with keys,

and with each jolt of the car the birthday girl flinches,
because she is on edge, she's celebrating
by signing herself into an adult locked ward,

this lovely young woman pretending to be invisible,
who has dressed for the party only to disappear.

Family Meeting

Ordinarily Dr. Rosen sprawls
in the chair across the room from mine.
He stretches his legs straight out.
He pulls off his glasses, rubs his eyes.
He's a bulky man. I can't imagine clothes
that would look right or comfortable on him.
Even his hair sprawls from his head.

But at this family meeting, a month
since I've been in the Institute,
he sits up straight, feet on the floor.
My parents sit on a sofa
I've never noticed before.
I pick at a tiny pattern of squares
on the right arm of my chair.
There's a discharge plan to discuss.

My doctor is in charge in this room.
He advises *a moratorium on pressure.*
He asks for my developmental history,
then the family history.
Now my mother makes her move.
My father committed suicide in 1946.
Bud's nephew committed suicide in 1971.

History clamps down on me.
My death sentence glares from both sides.
Dr. Rosen turns his wide face to me,
says, *I didn't know this.*
I tell him, only him, *Neither did I.*

Funhouse

not a turnstile/a trapdoor
not The Splash/The Cyclone
no stepping off
The Merry-Go-Round
you stay after dark
in this playground

popcorn soaked in Thorazine
lithium-laced cotton candy
The Thunderbolt's
for emergencies
The Tunnel of Love
is your dead end

Bumper Cars
The Penny Arcade
everything hurts
on this Roller Coaster
call the guards
they strap you tighter

no one's safe
on our Ferris Wheel
the view from the top
sends you crashing down
fireworks pop
in each boy and girl

not a picnic/a bad scene
not a day trip/a locked ward
only a funhouse
with a freak show
only a permanent detour

Hurting

The pros knew the ins and outs of sharps
and razor blades. Short sleeves displayed
their laddered stripes and stitchwork.
Nurses ran to rescue those who'd gone too far.
I climbed the ropes of Privileges, stopped
carving up my skin so I could graduate
to Grounds, with freedom to collect shards of glass
glinting on the generous lawns. Each time I sprang
a bloody leak I asked for help, a doctor to sew
my wounds, put the flesh back where it belonged,
circle my wrists in white gauze.

Often I lay face-up on linoleum and banged
my head. Sometimes I pummeled my chest
until I cried. Once I found a tiny hole
in a window screen and worried it until loose wires
cut my fingertips. Nearly a year spent in a trance
of violent loathing, yet I can't remember why I did
these things. My fingertips don't show a trace.
The scars on my arms remain, messy and confused.

I was only ever an amateur at suicide. For most
of a year I saw the pros come and go and die.
I told Dr. Rosen on a rare good day,
Someday I'll be glad I couldn't kill myself.
How did I know this, lost as I was? I knew it,
as certain as blood knew its way through my veins.

Primal

My mother takes the subway and a long bus ride
from work, elevator to the fifth floor. I sit slumped
in the lounge, not permitted to be in my room.
She hates being here. I do too, and I hate seeing her.

She doesn't think I belong in that soft vinyl chair,
spacious lounge, view of the grounds, clean room.
Now she sees my bandages, white, fraying bracelets.
You just have to do what everyone else is doing!

The blast of my scream murders her for a little while.
Red rises in my eyes, people run over, drag me away
still screaming, or maybe it's only echoes of screams
from other rooms sounding down the hall.

George's Big Night

Yelling, sloshing, alarms shrieking, feet running.
We startle awake in rooms off the glaring hallway,
stand barefoot in doorways, pajama cuffs rolled.
Gigantic George stands naked in the waters,
crazy geysering off his drooping flesh.

He'd yanked the water fountain from the wall.
A pipe gushes glacial water past our rooms
and George bellows, spouting sweat and spit,
shaking scary fists at a nurse no one likes.
He left his glasses on and nothing else.

Under the noise we speculate:
He must have cheeked his meds.
How can a fat man be so strong?
That's how mean we are. We like the spectacle.
Maintenance and Housekeeping race
onto the scene with a roaring vacuum cleaner.

The big male techs who specialize
in flaming madness fight George to the floor
and drag him to the locked and padded rooms
at the dead end of the hall. I've been there twice.
It's a desire I know well, to smash a dam
and flood the hallway of my night.

Friends on the Inside

We slouch on catty-corner sofas
beneath the Nurses' Station windows.
We're the *young adult patients*
of the fifth floor. We comment
on the passing scene, complain
about the staff, the rules, our doctors.
The guys spew long, resentful rants.

Zoned out on meds and chain-smoking,
exhausted from drugs and nothing to do,
our heads jangle or blank out.
Mine buzzes without purpose or worth.
The blandness of our talk irritates me,
exchanges of *I like* and *I hate* and gossip.
I'm not much help. I barely speak.

The lounge sofas and chairs
are arranged for *conversation*, but
much of the talk is with ghosts.
In my room I write down the accidental
poetry of overheard hallucinations.
Round tables in the dining area
are meant for *socialization*, often
a train wreck. Crying. Outbursts.
Heads on tables. Broken dishes.

But I find friends I can walk and talk
with on the grounds, around and around
the squared-off concrete path. At night
we pace the hall together. Friends here
come and go, get better, die, or get taken
elsewhere, but I remember. We offer
time and kindness to each other.
My mother warned me not to make friends
here, but where would I be if everybody's
mother had warned them off me?

Melvin

I drag a chair up to a window in the dining area.
It's clear enough tonight to see the crescent moon.
Most people are in bed, the lounge TV turned low.

Melvin is my favorite night shift psych tech.
He's assigned to me this evening.
I guess his task: draw me out, assess my state of risk.

He pulls a plastic chair up next to mine.
I trust his closeness, a man as short and young as I am.
His huge Afro is a halo, his speech casual and slow.

I tease Melvin about his stacked heel boots
and wide bell bottoms, his shiny purple disco shirt.
He came into work happy from an early date.

The question comes directly from his training:
What would you like to be doing in five years?
I answer, too quickly, *I'd like to be dead.*

I'm ashamed of my honesty even as I say it,
but that's why I'm here, my friend, at a dead end.

I've Never Told It Before

Lauren was beautiful, tall, long straight hair
and carved face, I think brown eyes. She sat
with a disgruntled group of my friends smoking
on the lounge couches. She wore hip huggers,
bell bottoms with frayed hems, always bare feet.
Sometimes she screamed and had to be restrained.

She took me into her confidence, me, quiet,
nearly mute, in overalls I embroidered
with a rainbow. We walked the shiny hallway
up and down. It was acid flashbacks, LSD,
she couldn't help what was happening to her head,
it was all a bad trip and she hated this place.

Exotic stuff next to my humdrum major depression.
Her intelligence darted, she had cutting things to say
about the doctors, nurses, psych techs, other patients.
It was heady. I lived in the fog in my head, hardly
seeing out. But people have always told me things.

One day Lauren told me, in agony, *It's like there's*
cotton stuffed in my head. I can't stand it anymore!
I couldn't stand my head either. I shared my plan.
Unscrew the light bulb in the lamp by your bed.
The lamp's screwed down but you can get the bulb.
Wrap it in a towel, smash it. Use a piece to cut yourself.

That night she did it, at least I think she died,
I don't remember if they told us, but I do remember
knowing why the nurses and techs ran
to Lauren's room and slid her off unconscious
to the hospital, and the smokers and I stood by
to watch in the lounge with the evening news on
and Housekeeping came with buckets and mops
and none of us wanted to talk.

Dalliance

David and I sit outside in winter coats
at dusk on our favorite bench. He's unfazed
by my secret escape plan. I can't keep a secret.
I can't keep living. I've faked my way
to Grounds Privileges to execute my plan.

During shift change next Thursday I'll ask
a nurse to let me off the floor for my session
with Dr. Rosen in his basement office.
I'll walk out the front entrance, walk three miles
to 30th Street Station, buy a pack of razor blades
at the station drugstore, buy a one-way ticket
on the Chestnut Hill Line to Kitchen's Lane.
I'll walk to Devil's Hole in Fairmount Park.
Hidden in the woods, I'll know just what to do.

David's pleased. *You're in love with death!*
He kisses me, full on, first and last time,
his crazy half-blind eyes closed,
his tobacco stink and body smell too close,
but David is my confidant and friend.
He thinks my plan is beautiful. It turns him on.

§

I follow all these steps methodically,
sick with fear of being caught and stopped.
It's cold and misty. The woods welcome me.
I hollow out a deathbed in the leaves.

I know what to do but it hurts too much.
I hack and slice and bleed but not
enough and there are park guards
on horseback, an ambulance, a hospital—
not mine—then my hospital again,
with no privileges at all.

51

Young Tree

O tree I prayed to
through a sealed window,
through a steel screen.
I traced your branches
through four seasons.
The television screamed,
the people slumped and raved.
I knew you, lovely one,
from five floors up.
God spoke from your
buds and leaves
to remind me I was still alive,
to urge me to rise up,
my tender captive tree.

Delancey Street Blues

You find your boyfriend's works
hidden in a desk drawer—burnt spoon,
matchbook, syringes, tourniquet. Somehow
you didn't notice he was always nodding off.
You've listened to his slurred stories,
sketched him in that state.

In the hospital he had looked like salvation,
his tragic limp, slow drawl, vampire-pale
resemblance to Dylan. Older than you. Sexy.
He knew the ropes, he had connections.
You perked right up when he came courting,
didn't you, babe? Your ticket out, your ticket
punched. You didn't wonder what a man like that
was doing with you, did you? Why he was broke?
He, a carpenter, you, his sad-eyed lady.

You rent a crummy apartment on Delancey
for the two of you. You get on disability.
Your check pays the rent. Your food stamps
buy the groceries. It's your furniture, dishes,
your everything. Your mattress on the floor.
You drag a cart each week to the laundromat.
You run so many errands for him!
Get books about Nazis at the library.
Get a special knife he wants. Get paregoric
when he finds another Yellow Pages doctor
who will call in a script. Idiot girl,
can't you figure out what that's a fix for?
You get tired of shopping, cooking,
errands, cleaning, taking orders.

He's got a system. Every night, after the news,
he gives you a Quaalude *to help you sleep.*
Good medicine for doubts. Good cover
for shooting up. You tell no one.
He teaches me so many things, he can be kind,
he's had a hard life, we love each other.
Coward, you're afraid to be alone.

You find his works.
You slam the drawer.
Your mind clicks into place.
Out he goes, without arguing or begging.
On the stairs he turns and says,
Don't ever let anybody take advantage
of you again. You got that, babe?

Caesura

Hold them cheap / May who ne'er hung there
      —Gerard Manley Hopkins

I have died, but not enough.
The petals that fall, the tears that don't.
Such a dizzy fall down from my window.
Dying geraniums in a window box.
What a long time it takes to form a word.
Dust lines my lips, rust coats my tongue.
I am alone in a bloody soup, thin soup.

I'll be a log in a stack of firewood.
I'll roll downhill in a barrel.
Life is taking too long.
Dust on my hands, rust on my feet.
Tears puddle in my ears.
Day after day in a barrel,
blinds drawn.

Thief

I wake up vomiting Judy's lithium on the blankets.
Martin thinks I'm sick but I know better—
not so sick I don't confess what's in that mess,
the pills I stole from Judy's medicine cabinet yesterday
before hugging her goodbye, before he walked me home.

Martin knows what I want to do and thwarts me,
reads to me, reasons with me, makes love to me.
I've outsmarted him, but the pills I gulped before sleep
are in a stinking half-digested heap and sticking to my hair.
I'm passing in and out, sick with failure.

Ambulance, stomach pump, bucket by the gurney.
A resident brings coffee: *Why did you do this, Joan?*
I say, *I'm not finished*, knowing what he'll have to do.
Stupid to refuse medication in measured daily doses.
Stupid to thieve it for another run at death.

It Kept Happening

I watch, and am as a sparrow alone upon the housetop.
　　　　　　　　　　　　　　　　　—Psalm 102:7

I walked to work before dawn. I had a key.
Something had gone wrong with a boyfriend.
Doesn't matter. I was supposed to be better.

I climbed circular stairs past our second-floor office,
then up to the third floor, then opened a window
and climbed onto the roof. No one to stop me.

I stood at that ledge for so long, close enough to sway,
close enough to eye the narrow walkway to the church
where my broken skull would lie.

What held me at the edge was a vision of my parents
staring at the mess of me. I hadn't seen that when I
wrote my note. It had seemed cleaner. The sun rose.

How did this look from a few buildings away? Not good
to the two men yelling from their apartment window
at International House. Was I okay? Did I need help?

To shut them up I climbed inside, slunk down the stairs
and to my desk, where an ordinary Monday had begun.
The police showed up. I was neither dead nor safe.

I Can't Stand It

I am in mourning for my life.
                    —Anton Chekhov

beside myself
not myself
the ghost I am
walking winter streets
tonight, tonight
tomorrow, tomorrow

thin, distracted
why sleep?
why bother waking up?
wash my clothes
eat a meal
comb my hair

the face I wear
a shadow of shame
for loving myself
in a bedrock way
too kind to
murder my life

Keep Her Safe

follow her down dark streets
draw men's bodies away
guard her door

keep her from rooftops
and speeding trucks
keep pills in their bottles

praise each drawn breath
and shaky exhale
beat in her heartbeats

hear her beg
be with me
answer, *I am here*

keep her safe
give her peace,
give her sleep
Lord, send rescue

Benediction

The ailanthus tree
in the back alley
crowds the window
of another building
where I hope to die.
Tree of Heaven,
city dweller,
I hurl my gaze
into your canopy,
trace outlines
of your silent leaves.

No One Knows About This

At night the trees lie down to rest.
They unclench their roots, groan,
and all sink down.
It makes a dry, rough sound.
They face the moon.
Their twigs sometimes break off,
the older branches don't.
Trees mesh with other trees
to make a high, dense stack.
At sunrise they rustle,
yank themselves upright.
Some leaves get lost.
They twist to get the angle right
and dig in for the day.

This One Day

One day, one day, this one day.
                        —Betty Adcock

Which morning did I wake safe from myself?
A Tuesday in May?
My December birthday?

Curtains tugged aside, sunrise or later,
floor beneath my feet,
a lifetime cracked open to old age.

In one breath I could stand it.
The only plan I had was breakfast
and all the breakfasts ahead.

In years to come I would choke in gray waters,
but I'd never sway on that ledge again, ever.

Drenched

There's no in between for a person like me,
only up or down, drowning or sitting pretty
in the lifeguard's chair, tooting my whistle,
declaiming and super-brave.

There's the Diving Tank or the Kiddie Pool,
no Adult Swim. No designated lanes.
Admire me in my bikini on the high dive,
blindfolded and in love at the same time.

I was born without a snorkel or a skin.
No dry land, no lessons, just jump in.

ONLY NOW

Being alive is not the same thing as being wrong.

—Luong Tran

The Day I Walked on Fire

it wasn't fire
it was ginkgo leaves
the sun lit them yellow
they were juicy with heat

the day I walked on ginkgo leaves
I imagined they were fire
that my shoes were melting
that my feet were burning

and I felt no pain
on that autumn day
when I burned to be
a holy woman

Romance

Death, my familiar, my handsome
intruder, we had a long run, didn't we?
Girlhood flirtation, frantic debauchery
until I betrayed you, my dear.
Recall how demanding you were.

Life frees me, asks nothing, stays
in the background, gives the lightest
of kisses. Do I miss you? Remember,
we fit exactly, I can't resist you,
I'll return someday. Wait for me.

December 2002

Click and puff of Dad's air hunger at the end.
On our last evening side by side he asked
to watch *My Fair Lady*. Dad in striped pajamas,
tubing looped around his too-long ears, poor man
surviving on morphine, thin air, and pudding.

Pompous Rex Harrison, Edwardian London,
and violets tied in bunches clasped
in Audrey Hepburn's elegant, dirty hands.
My poor Daddy, frail as a sparrow,
strained to stay awake and sing along.

All I want is a room somewhere
far away from the cold night air
warm face warm hands

Loverly Daddy far far away

Bud Speaks Up

Being born was the easy part (for me).
                              —Bud Freeman

What can I say? All my life I've suffered in silence
and played the clown. I was always quick with a joke
or a funny story. Now that I'm dead, if you think
I know what to say, you're mistaken.

I listened in on my memorial service at the Ethical
Culture Society, speeches read from the stage,
then so many people stood up to say I was sweet,
a gentle man, kind and funny. Nobody said I was
disappointed in my life, but that's how it was—

because I was the fourth child, an accident, fifteen
months after Bob and my heart was called weak,
because my mother Rose was no kind of mother,
because I didn't get an education, The School
of Hard Knocks they called it, because I nearly died

from TB and open-heart surgery, and Elsie
resented that, because gentiles could see the horns
on my head, because my father was meek,
my mother a tyrant. Because I couldn't stop Elsie
from hurting Joanie and Mike. Because I was meek.

No one divorced in those days, too shameful,
a shanda. We had fun at times, we had laughs.
We loved the kids, that's the truth. I worked
my tail off to make a living. Elsie never kept
a job for long. She couldn't stop herself,
she had to be right, she had to top everyone.

When I had my last sickness, cancer from asbestos
making ships for the war, Elsie resented even that,
the attention I got from everyone, that was amazing.
People are strange! From way up here I can see she's
feeling sorry for herself, still giving the kids hell.

In the Hallway of the Hospice Facility

The night nurse asks,
Have you considered PT for your mother?
I play her straight man.
What's the point of PT?
She can't even feed herself!
The nurse says, *No, PT, Pillow Therapy.*
A lot of families inquire about it.
We laugh and she lays a hand on my wrist,
not to take my pulse, but to link us
for a moment, daughters of mothers.

My pulse slows. I resume my vigil
beside the helpless, snoring figure.
This afternoon my mother froze out
the hospice chaplain, turned her head away
from his offer to pray with her. She spoke
instead to me: *Does he think he can*
convert me this late in the game?

Her Breath

Mike and I exchange a glance
over her cooling body.
Our eyes are dry.
Elsie wears a faded housedress
with a pattern of flowers.
Thirty minutes ago
an aide crossed
her swollen hands.

All morning we sat waiting
while Death rattled her.
She died in the afternoon
while we were out walking.
Our mother took a long, slow
rollercoaster ride to this day,
dragging us with her on
every shivery dip and climb.

Back from the dead,
Mike said, when she woke
from a coma, angry to find herself
in a spotless hospice room.
She raged until he put her back home.
Frail, sick, ninety-three,
hanging on ten years after Dad's death.
She scolded me yesterday.
I was late for lunch.
I had forgotten to pick up her mail.

Three months ago
their old bed was replaced
by a narrow hospital bed
rolled in by hospice workers
while she fumed in the living room
and I boiled water for tea.
Now her jaw is slack,
her last silent treatment.
Above her head hangs
the sad-eyed portrait of me at ten,
painted in blues and greys.

Elsie Has Her Say

Rube, Joe, and I started school speaking Yiddish.
The Italian kids told us the Jews killed Christ. Catholics,
very ignorant. My mother sewed my clothes and kept me
in Shirley Temple curls like a doll. No dresses off the rack
for me, and I wasn't allowed treif dinners at gentile houses.

I never got a fair shake. I could have gone to conservatory
for piano but the little money they had was for Rube
to study business at Wharton. I had to get a job. Rube
lorded his degree over me, believe you me! Joseph,
the favorite, died in the War. My father never got over it.

It took me three years and an operation to get pregnant
with Joanie. We wanted a baby so badly, our friends with
seconds and thirds. My first child at thirty-two! Michael
less than two years later. I wanted a boy first to name him
after my brother Joe. Joan stands for Joseph anyway.

Joanie never guessed it was me who found my father
on the kitchen floor, gas hissing, oven door open.
When she was in the Institute I spilled the beans
about his suicide. I put off her questions, but Joanie
never could let the past go. Water under the bridge.

She was a sweet little child but a sad young girl.
Her crying got on my nerves. I don't know what she had
to cry about, honestly. I grew up poor over my father's
tailor shop! So many times taking her to the pediatrician,
and the nurse calling me from school to get her.

Exasperating, and I let her know. I never was one
to hide my feelings. She thought her father was a saint,
but I knew better and told her so. The two of them always
laughing and joking. What's so funny? They were more
like brother and sister than father and daughter.

I didn't get married until I was twenty-seven,
still living under my mother's roof. Bud was my first
real boyfriend. But from the beginning Joanie was
too pretty for her own good. Boys, boys, boys, calling,
letters, dating, breaking curfew, what an ordeal.

Joanie is smart like my father, but no endurance.
Plenty of people are sad but they don't make such
a show of it. All we did for her and for years
she moped around, working jobs way beneath
her while Michael was making good money.

When Joanie had a family and Bud and I visited
he couldn't wait to get her to himself to complain
about me. I admit I did the same. Why not? She's
a grown woman and her husband is no saint either.
Bud was weak, never the man I wanted him to be.

Joanie and Mike loved Bud best. Everybody did,
no secret there. But after he was gone and I lived
ten years a widow with a hump back and a walker,
my kids did their duty, I'll give them their due.
Better than some women's kids I could name!

I didn't ask to live to such an age in such bad condition,
all kinds of women in the apartment taking care of me.
Too much time to think. Water under the bridge.

Grass Stains

Years ago, scrubbing the knees of my children's jeans,
muttering, as I did so, at the stubbornness of chlorophyll,
never at the backyard play that ground it in, play I could
watch with a glance out the kitchen window,

I summoned up my mother at the basement laundry sink,
deep galvanized tub—she, scouring city grime
from our clothes, bar of Fels Naptha at hand, stiff brush,
unshaded hanging bulb, worn sheets pegged to the lines.

My mother's ashes fill two black boxes,
one in an unused desk drawer at my house,
one on a basement shelf at my brother's.

Orange Tulips

My life (I joke with friends who see me
in the joke) tacks from shock to recovery,
pain to convalescence—ailments
of my aging body and invisible assaults
by lovers and the tempests of the outer world.

One night my silly darling cat died in the dryer,
mouth streaking blood across warm clothes.
The friend I asked to come over said, *I always
know where my cats are.* That night I lost both
cat and friend. Some recoveries are a snap.
That one took a summer, longer.

I wonder, do other people live like I do,
very bad to very good? Like the drooping
tulips in a vase I just gave cool water to.

Summer's Start

June's early fire draws up dawn,
light deepens the morning world.
It's cool before the dew burns off.
Mud in the ditch and leaves
on the road track last night's storm.
The afternoon will be hot.

My house is shaded, coddled by woods
as I am coddled by solitude.
I love this world I yearned to shed.
Dusk falls softly into the earth,
light drenches my reawakened life,
warms the small planet of my heart.

Acknowledgements

Birthing Age (Finishing Line Press): "No One Knows About This," "The Day I Walked on Fire," "Summer's Start"

Webster's Reading Room (Old Mountain Press anthology): "Word by Word"

Flying South: "Drenched"

Red Fez: "Caesura," "All Wrong," "Sore Throat"

The Power of Goodness (Chapel Hill Press anthology): "5905 Belmar Terrace"

The Main Street Rag: "Girl on a Bus," "Shame"

Kakalak: "Her Breath"

Hermit Feathers Review: "St. James Street," "Lullaby"

San Pedro River Review: "1963"

Speckled Trout Review: "This One Day"

Madness Muse Press: "Happy twenty-first," "Hurting," "George's Big Night," "Delancey Street Blues," "It Kept Happening"

"All Wrong" was nominated for Best of the Net by *Red Fez*. "Hurting" was nominated for a Pushcart Prize by *Madness Muse Press*.

Thank You

The Poet Fools, my critique group, deserves an award for slogging through the original versions of many of these poems. Thank you for your helpful comments. Thanks go to Judith Ferster and her exacting mother Dorothy, who critiqued an early version as a joint project. Thank you to Yvonne Monroe, Pam Baggett, Miriam Mills, and my cousin, Judy Freeman. Thank you to my brother, Mike Freeman, who recalled facts about our Philadelphia childhood I'd forgotten. Thank you always to my daughter and son, Clare and John, for their loving support.

At stages of writing this book, two readers gave me intensive critique. The first was J.S. Absher. We sat across a table with his generously notated copy. He confessed to never guessing this about me. It was hard to hold back tears. I realized three things that day: if this book were ever published it would be a personal coming out; readings would be challenging; my openness about mental illness would be accepted with kindness.

Michael Hettich's mentorship steered *Orange Tulips* beyond the fumbling stage into sharp focus. I'm baffled by the task of thanking him. I often thought myself incapable of making changes he suggested—then I became capable, a stronger poet. When I was discouraged by news from a publisher, he told me I was a true poet, something I suspected but had never hoped to hear.

About the Author

 Joan Barasovska lives in Orange County, North Carolina. For thirty-five years she has had a private practice in academic therapy, working with children with academic and psychological challenges. Joan cohosted a poetry series at the independent bookstore Flyleaf Books in Chapel Hill and serves on the Board of the North Carolina Poetry Society. In 2020 she was nominated for Best of the Net and a Pushcart Prize. Joan is the author of the chapbooks *Birthing Age* (Finishing Line Press, 2018) and *Carrying Clare* (Main Street Rag, 2022).

Author photo: Hannah Kitchin Stewart

Made in the USA
Columbia, SC
30 August 2024

40893688R00050